Crime in the Community

IRIS TEICHMANN

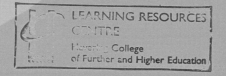

W
FRANKLIN WATTS
LONDON • SYDNEY

First published in 2002 by Franklin Watts
96 Leonard Street, London EC2A 4XD

Franklin Watts Australia
56 O'Riordan Street
Alexandria, NSW 2015

Series editor: Rachel Cooke
Series design: White Design
Picture research: Diana Morris

A CIP catalogue record for this book is available from the British Library.

ISBN 0 7496 4439 7

Dewey Classification 364

Printed in Belgium

Acknowledgements:
Giusseppe Bizzarri/Sipa/Rex Features: 19t. Robert Brook/Photofusion: 7, 15.
Lee Celano/Sipa/Rex Features: 27. Photo by Chat Magazine/Model released/Rex Features: 10.
Nigel Dickinson/Still Pictures: front cover. Paul Doyle/Photofusion: 11t, 11b.
Steve Eason/Photofusion: 13. Jonathan Evans/Reuters/Popperfoto: 8t.
David Gray/Reuters/Popperfoto: 5. Sally Greenhill/Sally and Richard Greenhill: 6tr, 24.
H.H.A./Rex Features: 16. Ian Hodgson/Reuters/Popperfoto: 23t.
David Hoffman/Still Pictures: 26b. Mitch Jacobson/Sipa/Rex Features: 12b.
Marty Katz/Rex Features: 20. Paul Lowe/Network: 26t.
Mike McWilliam/Photofusion: 28. Peter Olive/Photofuson: 9. Reuters/Popperfoto: 22t.
Rex Features: 4, 6bl, 8b, 17. Simon Roberts/Rex Features: 14.
Harmut Schwarzbach/Still Pictures: 18, 19b. Ian Simpson/Photofusion: 12t.
Sinopix/Rex Features: 21. The Sun/Rex Features: 22b.
Jeff Topping/Reuters/Popperfoto: 25. Bob Watkins/Photofusion: 29.

Whilst every attempt has been made to clear copyright should there be any inadvertent
omission please apply in the first instance to the publisher regarding rectification.

CONTENTS

WHAT DO YOU THINK about when you hear the word 'crime'? Your favourite crime novel? The latest episode of your favourite police drama on television? Or a recent news report of a shocking murder? We are all very aware of crime today.

HEARING ABOUT CRIME

It is not just the television news that reminds us of the reality of crime. Many local newspapers are full of headlines like: 'Elderly Woman Viciously Attacked at Home' or 'High Street Bank Robbed Again'. The sudden sound of police sirens can alert us daily to the existence of crime. Maybe you have seen police notices about particular crimes in your area.

FIRST-HAND EXPERIENCE

It is not just through the media we learn about about crime. Most of us know at least one person who has been directly affected by crime. Maybe you or one of your friends has had a mobile phone snatched, or had your home broken into. You or your family may have been a victim of violent crime. If this is the case, you will know at first-hand the distress crime causes.

A SOCIAL CONCERN

But even if we have no direct experience of crime, we are reminded of its threat every day. Your parents probably tell you not to stay out late or never to talk to strangers. The police give talks in schools to raise awareness about crime in the area. Governments talk about the scale of crime and what they intend to do about it. Public opinion polls also suggest that most of us consider crime and crime prevention to be two of the most important issues in our society today.

◀ *Only 10 years old, Damilola Taylor was murdered for no apparent reason in a street near his home. His death made headline news worldwide and highlighted concerns about crime in the community.*

↑ *In 1996, a man went on a shooting spree in Port Arthur, Tasmania in Australia, killing 35 people. A policewoman covers her face after leaving the café where the shooting took place.*

WHAT IS CRIME?

It seems obvious: a crime is any action or behaviour that is against the law. However, laws vary from country to country and are constantly changing. Crime breaks down into two main types. Violent crime includes murder, sexual assault, physical assault and robbery. Property-related crime covers any form of theft, from pick-pocketing and car theft to full-scale burglary, serious fraud and crimes that damage other people's property. There are many other actions that may be either criminal or simply unacceptable behaviour, such as traffic offences, being a noisy neighbour or vandalism.

WHAT DO YOU THINK?

- Do you think about crime in your area?
- Would you describe your area as safe?
- Does crime in the news affect how you think about crime in your area?
- What type of crime worries you the most and why?
- What precautions do you or friends of yours take against crime?

SHOULD WE BE WORRIED *about crime in our community? This question concerns us all as community crime can directly affect the quality of our lives. Our shock about a murder case reported on national television may not last for long. However, crime committed close to our doorstep can literally scare us.*

TOP COMMUNITY CRIMES

The most common types of crime that affect our neighbourhoods are theft and burglary. Elderly people are often seen as particularly vulnerable as they are less able to defend themselves. In fact statistics show that young people and single adults are more likely to be burgled.

⬇ *House burglaries are one of the most common types of crime worldwide.*

➡ *A lone woman walks down a quiet urban walkway. An opportunity for crime?*

OPPORTUNITIES FOR CRIME

Areas with lots of shops and restaurants, or poorly lit areas – like shortcuts to train and bus stations – particularly attract thieves. Robbery rates are especially high in shopping streets without security cameras or regular police patrols. Local businesses may decide to close if they are the victims of too much crime.

COMMUNITY CONCERNS

Today, many local residents complain about young people behaving badly, particularly in deprived areas. In such areas, graffiti on the walls or damage to houses or cars is distressing as it destroys the surroundings and lowers the quality of life. It also attracts more crime.

VIOLENCE AND DRUGS

Today people also worry about the scale of drug abuse and drug-related crime, which used to be associated with deprived areas or housing estates in bigger towns or cities. Yet nowadays signs of drug abuse can be seen anywhere. We may find used drug syringes in our local park or read in our local paper about drug addicts dying of an overdose. Drugs are very expensive so much violent crime surrounds the drug-dealing business.

⊕ *In run-down and deprived areas, crimes such as graffiti and vandalism are commonplace.*

FACING THE ISSUES

All of us face the issue of crime:

Ingrid, parent, Sydney, Australia: "We are constantly afraid of being burgled. Someone has tried to break into our house... We also had our car stolen. It was used for other thefts and then dumped. I think most thefts are down to drug addicts."

Ria, single, London, UK: "I see more notices about crime around these days, but I don't really think that crime is worse. I've never been a victim, luckily. More patrols on the street would be good – I think that puts criminals off more than anything."

James, married, New York, USA: "Just about everyone I know has had a wallet or purse stolen. It's an everyday hazard. I live with it. In fact, New York feels a lot safer today, but I still don't use the subway late at night."

SURVEYS SHOW THAT *the general public often thinks that crime is increasing when official crime statistics for reported crime show that the opposite is true. Why is this? Somehow many people are forming a biased view of the level of crime.*

MEDIA COVERAGE

The media plays a major part in the way we think about crime. National television stations and newspapers usually only focus on crime if a famous person is involved, if the crime is particularly horrific, or if the crime challenges the way in which the police or justice system work. Local and regional television and press, however, increasingly use crime to attract people's attention. In Canada, for example, some television stations were found to devote as much as 50 per cent of their programmes to crime.

Children are walked to school after the murder of a local child. News of crime makes us all more careful.

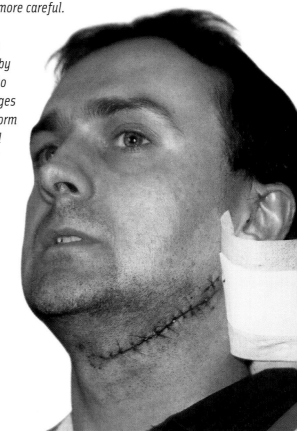

This man was stabbed by car thieves. Do shocking images like these inform us or help sell newspapers?

SENSATIONALISM

An American regional news director once said, "When somebody's killed, that's news." In a country like the United States where local television stations compete fiercely for viewers, violent crime is seen as particularly attention-grabbing. Coverage of violent crimes in the United States has increased at a time when the number of murders has actually gone down.

LOCAL ISSUES

Local newspapers try to reflect the concerns of their community in order to sell more copies. A recent study on the way in which the national and local Australian press covered drugs and crime showed that in the mid-1990s, when drugs and crime were felt to be mainly a problem for big cities, the local press outside these urban areas rarely covered such issues. Coverage increased dramatically, however, as the use of illegal drugs and drug-related crime started to become a concern at local level as well.

➡ *A murder provokes grief and anger in any community. Media coverage reflects this.*

GET THE FACTS STRAIGHT

These are the latest available statistics of the actual rise and fall of types of crime (all for the year 2000 except Australian ones which are for 1999) based on police records:

	Australia	USA	Germany	UK
Murder	+15%	-0.1%	-2.8%	+4%
Assault	+2%	-0.1%	+2.1%	+3.4%
Robbery[1]	-5%	-0.4%	-3.3%	+12.9%
Burglary[2]	-5.8%	-2.4%	-6.1%	-7.8%
Drugs	+8.3%	+0.02%	+7.8%	-6.9%

1. Theft where violence or the threat of violence is used
2. Theft by breaking into someone else's property

PUBLIC REACTION

For many of us, the media is usually the only source of information about crime in our area. If we are always hearing about murders or robberies, we may decide that it is no longer safe for our children to play outside or walk to school on their own. Some people feel that we overreact and that unnecessary fear results in a loss of personal freedom. Most though see it as taking sensible precautions and that it is "better to be safe than sorry".

REPORTING CRIME

NO ONE WANTS TO become a victim of crime and, indeed, the chance of becoming the victim of a serious crime is very low. However, what would you do if your bag got stolen in the street? Would you go after the thief or would you be too shocked to react? Would you go immediately to the nearest police station to report the theft?

⬇ *Many people do not report a crime such as bag snatching as they feel the police are unlikely to solve it.*

THE SCALE OF HIDDEN CRIME

If we do not report a crime to the police, it will remain unrecorded and will not appear in the official crime statistics. Governments rely heavily on these statistics to discover how bad crime is across the country, and to look at ways in which to tackle it. Unreported crime is called hidden crime and it is a big problem for governments.

Most countries provide victim support groups to help crime victims to come to terms with their experiences.

ASHAMED, OR AFRAID?

Even some serious crimes are not reported. A woman subjected to a sexual assault may be too ashamed to tell the police about what has happened. In fact, statistics for most developed countries show that victims of sexual offences are least likely to go to the police. In European countries, an increasing number of immigrants and asylum seekers have recently experienced racial abuse and attacks. Many do not report the incident because they are afraid of their attackers or because they think the police may not take their case seriously. Some feel that the police themselves are racially prejudiced.

Police forces around the world try to promote a friendly and accessible image, but many crime victims feel the police will not give them a sympathetic response.

WHY NOT REPORT?

Whether we report a crime mostly depends on what crime it is and how serious it is. In most countries, the majority of reported crimes are thefts and burglaries. In fact, there are signs that people are increasingly willing to report a theft. However, research by the Australian government still finds that many people do not report the crime because they think either it is not important, or the police cannot do anything. Some people even think that they can sort it out themselves.

WHO COMMITS CRIME?

MANY OF US HAVE CERTAIN groups of people in mind when we think of criminals and thugs. Local residents tend to blame young people for petty crime and vandalism in their community. In Western countries, black people are often blamed for crime. We tend to associate certain types of white adult men with disorderly or even violent behaviour in our community. Are these stereotypes backed up by the facts?

MALE MAJORITY

Statistics suggest that men are committing far more crimes than women. For example, in the year 2000, over 90 per cent of people arrested in the United States were men. The number of women committing crimes is gradually increasing but women are more likely to commit property-related rather than violent crimes.

⬆ These youngsters are simply "hanging out". Yet some locals may well brand them as potential criminals.

⬇ In the United States, contrary to public belief, only a very small proportion of Latin Americans commit crimes.

⬆ *Statistics show that the majority of convicted criminals are white, male and at least in their mid-twenties.*

YOUNG AND DANGEROUS?

Why are young teenagers blamed for crime when statistics show that only a minority of those convicted of a crime in Western countries are under the age of 18? High-profile cases of young killers, such as the two boys who killed the two-year-old James Bulger in England in 1993, fuel levels of anxiety. But it may be that young people promote this image simply by hanging out on the street and playing loud music.

A QUESTION OF COLOUR?

Are people from ethnic minorities more likely to commit a crime? Statistics do show that black people in the United States and Britain, for example, are far more likely to be arrested and put into prison than white people. But the statistics do not show the whole picture. Some experts point out that young black people are more likely to live in deprived areas subject to government crack-downs on crime.

GET THE FACTS STRAIGHT

- Men between the ages of 18 and 25 are most likely to commit a crime. They are also the group most likely to become a victim of crime.

- A recent survey of prisoners in London showed that over 50% were unemployed, 45% had been unemployed for more than two years, 46% had no qualifications and 56% were on state benefits.

- In Australia, indigenous people are 14 times more likely to be put in prison than white Australians.

- The latest US prison statistics show that 36% of inmates had been unemployed and 20% were looking for work. 66% had been in prison before.

- In the United States, 63% of the prison population are from ethnic or racial minorities, even though the majority of crime is committed by white people.

WHY COMMIT CRIME?

CAN YOU *imagine any reasons why you might commit a crime? Do you know anyone who has been involved in shoplifting and enjoyed the thrill of not being found out? Would you ever be tempted to take your parents' money? There are many different and often complex factors that contribute towards a person committing a crime.*

POVERTY

In every society, people who are homeless or living in poor housing with very little money to spend are more likely to commit theft. In fact, theft is the most common type of crime all over the world. In some countries, even begging is a crime. Some people feel forced into crime to feed their families.

RICH VERSUS POOR

There are signs that the gap between rich and poor in some Western countries is increasing rather than decreasing. This causes a lot of envy. Many people who are dependent on state welfare live in poor housing, where there are few employment and education opportunities available to them. With little chance of improving their way of life, some people turn to crime to do just this.

FACING THE ISSUES

Drug dependency can lead people to crime (see pages 18-19). Stuart is a 25-year-old from Glasgow. He has a long history of selling and using drugs, and has also committed robbery and assault. "You don't realise how bad you are until you're not using, and then you can see what you were like and how much of an idiot you were. But you don't realise it at the time."

After a recent arrest, Stuart was surprised to be given the chance of treatment outside of prison. "It's a brilliant idea," says Stuart. "Like myself now, I'm not just straight, I'm at college ... and I'm going to do a degree. I want to get a job in graphic design. I have a life now, a different life. There are people like me in and out of jail through drugs, and they're not getting any help. This has changed my life, and it could change other people's lives if they really want to do it."
[Source: BBC]

OUR ENVIRONMENT

People who live in run-down and neglected residential areas may become increasingly dissatisfied with their living conditions. As a result, vandalism, burglary, muggings and car crime often increase. People are also more likely to use drugs. Despite this, it is important to remember that most people do not actually turn to crime, however disadvantaged their lives may be.

◀ *Youths show off by vandalising a car. Boredom and lack of off-street meeting places can lead to crime.*

CRIME CHANGES

Crime statistics change constantly and there are many types of crime not associated with poverty and social exclusion. In times of economic prosperity, violent crimes and crimes against women, for example, tend to be higher than property-related crimes. A lot of violent crimes committed by men are thought to have been committed simply because they were bored or wanted to impress others or show that they were strong and brave.

◀ *A neglected environment and poverty are still the main factors contributing to crime today.*

VIOLENT CRIME

VIOLENT CRIMES ARE OFFENCES *of murder, sexual assault, violent robbery or assault against another person. They are very serious crimes indeed and they attract the toughest sentences. Although levels of violent crime are much lower than other types of crime, the police tend to give these crimes priority and the media devotes more time to reporting them.*

AN URBAN CRISIS

London has one of the richest populations in Europe. Yet 13 of its local boroughs are the poorest in the whole of the United Kingdom. During 1999 and 2000, 43 per cent of all crime in the United Kingdom and 27 per cent of all violent crime against another person were committed in London. There has recently been an increase in violent crime in the United Kingdom, contrary to trends in the United States, where the rates of violent crime have remained relatively stable.

THE ECONOMIC LINK

It is interesting to compare the United Kingdom's increase in violent crime at a time of economic prosperity with the general decline of violent crime in the United States during a time of economic recession. It may well be that people with already limited opportunities are least likely to benefit from a society with a booming economy, as they have not gained the experience or skills necessary to compete in an already competitive job market. This may make them not only feel violent but also less concerned about the consequences of being violent.

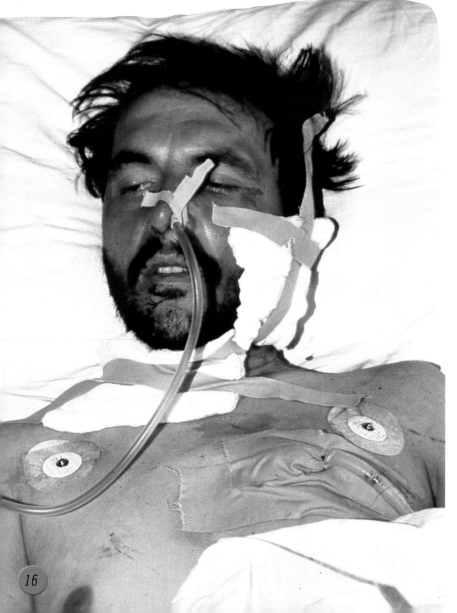

 This recently married man in Istanbul, Turkey, was stabbed by his own wife. Lesser violence in the home often goes unreported. Murder is often a "crime of passion".

 *A good night out does not always end happily. Violent crime is often linked in some way to alcohol or drug consumption.*

OTHER REASONS

Economic prosperity may cause some people who are employed and generally not associated with crime to commit violent crime. For example, many violent crimes are linked to an increase in drug or alcohol abuse, habits that require a good deal of money. Pride, solidarity with one's fellow men, frustration or rage can be other causes for people to commit a violent crime.

GET THE FACTS STRAIGHT

- On average, 2 in every 100,000 people are murdered in Australia, 1 in every 100,000 people in the United Kingdom and 30 in every 100,000 people in the United States.

- In Australia, the increase in the prison population is mainly due to an increasing number of people being arrested for violent crimes. (This does not mean, however, that violent crime has actually increased.)

- In the United States, the rate of violent crime in 2000 was at its lowest level ever.

- In the United States, 66% of murders involved the use of firearms, compared with only 19% in Australia.

THE DRUGS TRADE

THERE ARE AN ESTIMATED 190 million drug addicts and drug users worldwide. The illegal drugs trade is worth 400 billion dollars. The use of drugs is increasingly common among young people. Not surprisingly, drug-related crime is on the increase.

WHERE DO THE DRUGS COME FROM?

The farming, production and transport of illegal drugs take place far away from Western countries. Afghanistan is currently the largest producer of illegal drugs, which are transported west along various routes into Turkey. Other key production countries are Colombia and the Caribbean. Certain countries have emerged as key transit areas for illegal drugs. 60 per cent of drugs coming into the United States are distributed from Mexico, but they also arrive from Haiti and Nigeria.

GET THE FACTS STRAIGHT

More and more people use drugs for enjoyment. Like alcohol and cigarettes, drugs have a stimulating effect. However, drugs also have very serious side effects.

- Cannabis and Ecstasy: often presented as being less harmful than other drugs. They have serious long-term effects, particularly for young people's mental ability to think and remember.

- Cocaine and amphetamines: cause tremors, headaches, hypertension and increased heart rate. Long-term effects include nausea, insomnia, weight loss, convulsions and depression.

- Heroin: causes nausea, slow respiration, dry skin, itching, slow speech and slow reflexes. Over a long period of time there is a serious risk of developing physical and psychological dependence, which can result in acute overdose and even death due to respiratory depression.

  [Source: United Nations Office for Drug Control and Crime Prevention]

It is much more common for young people today to experiment with drugs than it was a decade ago.

⬆ *Drug addicts may leave used syringes lying around anywhere, and these can pose serious health hazards, particularly for children.*

⬇ *Drug-dealing provides a quick and easy, but dangerous, way of making money.*

WHO IS INVOLVED?

A handful of extremely wealthy people run the global drugs business. They hire large numbers of so-called 'middlemen' to arrange the deals and employ people to smuggle the drugs into the West, where demand is steadily growing.

THE CONSEQUENCES

Drug-dealing increases violence, particularly against those involved in the trade when deals go wrong or because of competition. As more drugs are used, drug-related crime inevitably goes up. Drugs change people's behaviour and drug addiction pushes people into crime in order to support their addiction.

IS THE POLICING WORKING?

Western countries have substantially increased the amount of money and police resources used to track down people involved in the drugs trade. Recent Australian research, however, mirrors the experience of other Western countries, suggesting that policing of drugs is not very effective and does nothing to stop the continued demand. Many people think that the use of soft drugs like cannabis should be made legal.

TODAY GUNS ARE *widely available, but do more guns mean more crime? The example of the United States seems to suggest so. The United States has one of the highest numbers of people owning guns in the Western world and one of the highest rates of gun-related crime. In Australia, however, the number of violent crimes involving firearms is surprisingly low despite a high level of gun ownership.*

⬆ *The arms trade is one of the biggest businesses in the world and in most countries it is very easy to get hold of a firearm.*

➡ *Armed police in Hong Kong, China arrest a member of the Triads, a criminal gang notorious for its use of violence.*

GANG-RELATED CRIME

In recent years, there have been many fatal shootings in some Western countries, particularly the United Kingdom, related to gang warfare. These shootings are carried out by groups of young men involved in importing and selling illegal drugs or guns, or in robberies in deprived inner-city areas. However, these groups are not well organised, and experts say that the public's fear of an American-style gun culture coming to the United Kingdom is exaggerated.

POLICE RESPONSE

Owing to the increase in shootings, armed police now patrol the streets in some areas of the United Kingdom. The police have also set up specific initiatives to target gun crime in those local areas most affected by gang warfare. Teams of police officers concentrate on gathering information on individuals involved in gangs and on building links with community leaders. However, the sight of armed police patrolling estates on a daily basis has caused anxiety among local residents.

SHOULD POLICE BE ARMED?

In countries like the United Kingdom, where police officers do not routinely carry guns, it is police officers rather than the public who think they should be armed to protect themselves better. However, there is no evidence from countries like the United States and France, whose police forces carry guns in public, that guns give more protection to police officers. Violent crime rates vary considerably irrespective of whether or not the local police are armed.

FACING THE ISSUES

Criminal gangs in the United Kingdom and some other countries have started to copy the ways of criminal gangs in Kingston, Jamaica. Gang members love showing off their expensive cars and jewellery. They create respect based on fear and do not hesitate to kill their own members for lack of loyalty or misbehaviour. They also kill rival gang members as they compete for business opportunities selling guns, but mostly drugs. They do not seem to care about dying young. For some young people, gang life can be very attractive: not only does it bring power but it also offers excitement, a sense of belonging, potential wealth and a way of standing out from the crowd.

RACIAL CRIME

IN THE UNITED STATES, the racially-motivated murders of James Byrd and Matthew Shepard shocked the nation. In the United Kingdom, the murder of the teenager Stephen Lawrence radically challenged the way in which the police treated black people. In these cases, the black victims were initially seen as in some way to blame for their deaths. Many people view black and ethnic minorities as potential criminals and this discrimination can even stretch to the police and the courts.

➡ *Waterloo Road in Oldham, Britain, the day after violent clashes between white and Asian groups in May 2001.*

⬆ *The parents of the murdered black teenager Stephen Lawrence started a high-profile campaign against racial discrimination in the British police and justice system.*

THE SCALE OF RACIAL CRIME

Governments are beginning to realise that the scale of racial crime is worrying. Most racial harassment involves verbal abuse, verbal and physical intimidation and threats, sometimes leading to property damage or graffiti. With a rising number of immigrants and asylum seekers in Western countries there is a parallel rise in harassment or worse. In Scotland, a Kurdish asylum seeker was recently brutally stabbed to death on a housing estate in Glasgow.

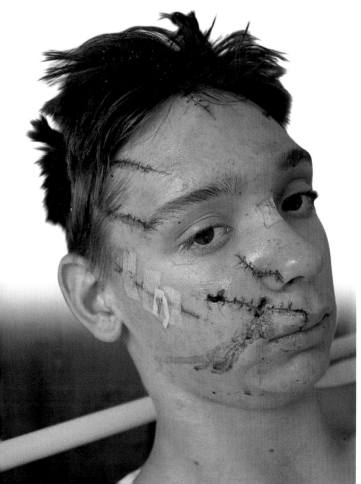

⬅ *This youngster was attacked because his friend is black.*

GET THE FACTS STRAIGHT

Here are some definitions of key words connected to the racism debate.

- Hate crime (United States): any unlawful action designed to frighten, harm, injure, intimidate or harass an individual because of the race, religion, ethnic or national origin, sexual orientation, gender or disability of the victim.

- Racial harassment (United Kingdom): a person is the victim of racial harassment if s/he has been attacked, insulted or intimidated because of his/her skin colour, race, ethnic or national origin.

- Racial vilification (Australia): any activity or behaviour which results in harassing people because of their colour, race, ethnicity or nationality.

Any such acts are illegal.

REPORTING RACIAL CRIME

Statistics show that more racial crime is being reported but does that mean there is more racial crime? It is only a few years since the United States and the United Kingdom began to keep official records of racial incidents reported to the police. For many, however, reporting racial harassment is difficult. Asylum seekers may not speak the language or know where to go for help. Others don't report the incident because they know the police can only act when someone is physically harmed. Many indigenous Australians do not know that they can seek justice for racial harassment.

WHAT CAUSES THESE CRIMES?

Some evidence suggests that racial crime and harassment is more likely to occur in areas with high unemployment rates, or in areas where there are few people from black and ethnic minorities. Some experts think that people who show hostility towards others of different ethnicity and colour have a general fear of strangers or may display unhealthy levels of national pride to compensate for their lack of success in society.

WHAT CAN GOVERNMENTS DO?

ONE OF THE KEY *responsibilities of any government is to maintain law and order. As crime is a major concern for most of us, we tend to associate an increase in crime with the government's failure to keep crime under control. But why do governments continue to want to show that they are tough on crime, when statistics suggest that the crime rates overall have not increased significantly?*

⬇ *Community sentences, such as these two offenders are serving, are often seen as being 'soft on crime', but fewer people reoffend after doing them than after a prison sentence.*

THE ROLE OF THE MEDIA

As news coverage focuses on high-profile violent crime, we tend to get a distorted picture of the general level of crime. Most of us remain unaware of official crime statistics. Governments may know that a growing public fear of crime does not reflect a rise in actual crime, but they still need to be seen to act.

PUNISHMENT

One way of responding to the public's fear of crime is for governments to announce that they are going to be tougher on criminals. As a result, the courts can suddenly give harsher sentences to convicted criminals, or decide to put someone in prison where previously the offender would only have been given a fine or a community sentence.

↑ *In Phoenix, Arizona, in the United States, female prisoners work in a chain gang. Some think harsh treatment of prisoners prevents them from reoffending.*

DOES IMPRISONMENT WORK?

Although some Western countries have set up special units to carry out research into crime and crime prevention, the main thrust of criminal justice is still to put offenders in prison. The prison population in most Western countries has grown steadily in recent years. Prisons are extremely expensive to maintain and studies show that the majority of prisoners are likely to offend again once released.

WHAT DOES THE PUBLIC WANT?

Each of us wants to feel safe. But do governments' attempts at tougher measures against criminals make us feel safer? Opinion polls suggest that it is more likely that the public feels frustrated and disillusioned with the way the traditional justice system works. Given the choice, there are signs that most people would prefer to see proper measures in place to prevent crime and to educate young people about the dangers of crime, rather than the introduction of tougher measures to punish criminals.

WHAT DO YOU THINK?

- How would you go about finding out about crime prevention in your area?
- Do you think enough is being done?
- If there was one thing you could change to make you feel safer, what would it be?
- Do you think poster campaigns can be effective in raising awareness about the dangers of crime?

POLICING

CAN YOU IMAGINE WHAT would happen if there were no police to enforce law and order? Western countries spend billions of of their taxpayers' money every year on policing. But surveys show that most of us want to see even more police officers patrolling the streets.

POLICE RESOURCES

Crime problems in big cities may be similar, but police resources vary considerably. New York employs around 40,000 police officers compared with just over 25,000 in London, where the population is much the same. But even the wealthiest countries have limited resources and save money by allowing police officers to patrol on their own, rather than in pairs.

⬆ *For many of us, seeing police officers in uniform patrolling the streets in pairs is a reassuring sight, but we are unaware of the cost implications.*

⬇ *A visible police presence may help prevent street crime and antisocial behaviour, like cycling on the pavement.*

UNIFORM APPEAL

What do you think about a shopping mall being patrolled by a police officer in a Santa Claus outfit? Most of us probably feel more reassured by a police officer in uniform and governments agree.

In the United States, people are used to sitting next to police officers in uniform in fast-food outlets. This is not usual in Britain and the British government is still trying to convince its police force that the British public would not feel threatened by uniformed police in public places other than the local high street.

PLAIN CLOTHES POLICE

We probably associate police officers in plain clothes with detectives solving complex crimes. Governments also employ a small number of lower-rank police officers in plain clothes to catch criminals in places such as shopping malls, train or metro stations, or at big events, such as football matches.

CAN WE TRUST THE POLICE?

Unfortunately, not all of us feel that we can trust the police to treat us sympathetically and fairly. Black people are still more likely to be stopped and searched on the streets than white people. Young men are also more likely to be targeted by patrolling police officers than women. This can cause resentment and the belief that the police are picking on you. Maybe you have also heard of your local police using excessive force.

WHAT DO YOU THINK?

Research suggests that only about 30% of police time is spent responding to reports of crimes. Most police work is about reassuring and providing advice to the public, personnel management and managing disputes. Below are some of the core tasks of the police. Which ones do you think should have priority?

- Crime prevention and detection
- Traffic control and related matters
- Community relations and dealing with community problems
- Public reassurance and public order maintenance

Although the Los Angeles police here manage to arrest a criminal gang, only one in ten arrests actually leads to a criminal conviction.

MANY COMMUNITIES *particularly affected by crime have relatively well-off households in close proximity to poorer ones. They also often have a large number of people who depend on state welfare. Local councils in these areas normally have various initiatives in place to help prevent crime and to improve the environment in areas where most crime takes place.*

REGENERATION

Many recognise that the local environment can have a significant impact on crime and disorder. Generally, the more neglected and rundown a neighbourhood becomes, the more some people in the neighbourhood are likely to destroy it further with crime, graffiti and thoughtless behaviour. Communities can work with local councils and voluntary groups to start projects to clean up areas, to remove dumped vehicles and improve street lighting.

A cleaner, more pleasant environment that also provides recreational opportunities for young people can help to reduce crime.

VIGILANCE

Apart from police officers on the streets, installing security cameras has been shown dramatically to decrease the crime rates in high-risk areas. Unfortunately this can affect neighbouring areas if they do not have security cameras, as potential criminals are likely to go there to commit a crime with less risk of being caught. Some people disagree with too many cameras on the streets, arguing that this violates privacy rights.

NEIGHBOURHOOD WATCH

In the United Kingdom, Neighbourhood Watch schemes have existed since the early 1980s. They are community-based initiatives supported by the local police, whereby households agree to be vigilant and report any suspicious activities on their street to the police. Many feel these schemes help prevent crime. Surveys show, however, that most Neighbourhood Watch schemes, which cover 25 per cent of the country, are actually in low-crime rate areas anyway.

FACING THE ISSUES

One successful crime prevention initiative was set up by the Dutch Ministries of Justice, Employment and Education. They helped set up the 'City Guards Project', which employs long-term unemployed people to supervise and survey parking areas, shopping centres, housing estates and public transport. The project currently employs about 2,500 so-called 'City Guards', who are unemployed young people, to help create a safer environment and make the local community feel more secure.

⬆ *Surveillance cameras are a common sight in many Western cities.*

COMMUNITY PARTNERSHIPS

A key aspect of crime prevention nationally and locally is raising awareness about crime and community safety among all members of the community. Local councils together with teachers, police officers and parents can run workshops at schools to educate students about how to prevent crime, and to show them the dangers of getting involved in crime. These community projects are proving far more effective in implementing crime prevention measures than initiatives by national governments alone.

GLOSSARY

asylum seekers: People who have left their own country and applied for special protection called asylum or refugee status in another. Asylum is given to people who can prove that their lives are in danger because of the political situation in their own country.

burglary: Theft, usually by breaking into someone else's property.

crime statistics: Official government figures on the amount and types of crime that are reported to the police during a certain period of time.

discrimination: Reacting to people and treating them in a particular way, usually negative, because of their race, religion, nationality, gender, age or sexual orientation.

drug abuse: Misuse of drugs, particularly excessive use. Alcohol abuse is the excessive use of alcohol.

drug addicts: Usually refers to people who are dependent on illegal drugs and suffer severe physical discomfort if they stop taking them.

economic recession: A period when a country's economy (that is the amount of money it is making) is shrinking.

ethnic minorities: People who have a different cultural or racial background from mainstream society.

fraud: Criminally deceiving someone in order to gain from them, usually financially.

immigrants: People who have come into a country from another and settled there.

indigenous people: The people who are native to a country and have not immigrated there in the past few hundred years, such as the Aboriginal people in Australia.

justice system: Institutions and individuals that work to maintain law and order, such as the police, the courts, judges and lawyers.

mugging: A widely-used term for violent theft or robbery, particularly on the street. It is not one used in law.

murder: The act of illegally and intentionally killing another person; also called homicide.

offender: Someone who has committed a crime.

petty crime: Minor crime such as theft of little value, shoplifting or graffiti.

physical assault: Deliberately causing harm or injury to another person.

privacy rights: The rights people have to lead their lives without being watched by the state, the media or the public.

robbery: Theft where violence or the threat of violence is used.

sentence: In law, the punishment given by a judge to a convicted criminal.

sexual assault: Forcing sexual attentions on someone. When actual sexual intercourse occurs, the assault becomes rape.

state welfare: Support, usually money, given by the government to people in need.

stereotype: Something seen as a typical example of its kind.

truancy: Not attending school on a regular basis, even though legally required to do so.

vandalism: Deliberately destroying or damaging property belonging to another person or to the public.

Find further information about crime in the community on these websites. Most have good links to other sites.

GOVERNMENT SITES

Australia's Attorney-General's Department
Australian government department responsible for law and order. Links to individual Territories law and order departments, too.
www.law.gov.au

United Kingdom Home Office
The UK government office responsible for law and order. Site includes information on policy, statistics and advice.
www.homeoffice.gov.uk

United States Federal Bureau of Investigation
The FBI's site has information on its policy, links to statistics and a children's section.
www.fbi.gov

United States Bureau of Justice Statistics
Provides a wide range of statistical information related to crime in the USA.
www.ojp.usdoj.gov/bjs/

United States Department of Justice
US government department responsible for law and order. Site has a children's section.
www.usdoj.gov

CRIME AND CRIME PREVENTION

Australian Institute of Criminology
Government-financed but independent centre for the study of crime and criminal justice in Australia. Has useful statistical information.
www.aic.gov.au

Australasian Centre for Policing Research
Covering both Australia and New Zealand, researches police practices and develops new ideas, while promoting an international viewpoint.
www.acpr.gov.au

Justice Action
Australian community-based organisation, particularly concerned with the treatment of convicted criminals.
www.justiceaction.org.au

National Association for the Care and Resettlement of Offenders
NACRO is an independent UK voluntary organisation working to prevent crime and reoffending by criminals.
www.nacro.org.uk

International Victimology Website
Promotes the UN Declaration of the Basic Principles of Justice for Victims of Crime and the Abuse of Power.
www.victimology.nl

United Nations Crime and Justice Information Network
Statistics, information and global links about national and international crime.
www.uncjin.org

United Nations Office for Drug Control and Crime Prevention
Concerned with international policing of drug trafficking and its links with terrorism.
www.undcp.org

INTERNATIONAL LINKS

International Society of Crime Prevention Practitioners
A US site with links to local crime prevention groups.
www.crimeprevent.com/iscpp/links.htm

National Criminal Justice Reference Service – United States
Links to information about crime and drugs control.
www.ncjrs.org

International Crime Statistics Link Guide
Private website with strong international links section.
www.crime.org/links_intern.html

INDEX